AF235587

Introduction to the Darknet

Darknet 101

Martin Hoffer

Bibliografische Information der Deutschen Nationalbibliothek:

Die Deutsche Nationalbibliothek verzeichnet diese Publikation in der Deutschen Nationalbibliografie; detaillierte bibliografische Daten sind im Internet über http://dnb.dnb.de abrufbar.

Herstellung und Verlag: BoD –
Books on Demand, Norderstedt

ISBN: 978-3-7526-2972-9

Introduction

By using this book, you accept this disclaimer in full.

No advice

The book contains information. The information is not advice and should not be treated as such.

No representations or warranties

To the maximum extent permitted by applicable law and subject to section below, we exclude all representations, warranties, undertakings and guarantees relating to the book.

Without prejudice to the generality of the foregoing paragraph, we do not represent, warrant, undertake or guarantee:

- that the information in the book is correct, accurate, complete or non-misleading.

- that the use of the guidance in the book will lead to any particular outcome or result.

Limitations and exclusions of liability

The limitations and exclusions of liability set out in this section and elsewhere in this disclaimer: are subject to section 6 below; and govern all liabilities arising under the disclaimer or in relation to the book, including liabilities arising in contract, in tort (including negligence) and for breach of statutory duty.

We will not be liable to you in respect of any losses arising out of any event or events beyond our reasonable control.

We will not be liable to you in respect of any business losses, including without limitation loss of or damage to profits, income, revenue, use, production, anticipated savings, business, contracts, commercial opportunities or goodwill.

We will not be liable to you in respect of any loss or corruption of any data, database or software.

We will not be liable to you in respect of any special, indirect or consequential loss or damage.

Exceptions

Nothing in this disclaimer shall: limit or exclude our liability for death or personal injury resulting from negligence; limit or exclude our liability for fraud or fraudulent misrepresentation; limit any of our liabilities in any way that is not permitted under applicable law; or exclude any of our liabilities that may not be excluded under applicable law.

Severability

If a section of this disclaimer is determined by any court or other competent authority to be unlawful and/or unenforceable, the other sections of this disclaimer continue in effect.

If any unlawful and/or unenforceable section would be lawful or enforceable if part of it were deleted, that part will be deemed to be deleted, and the rest of the section will continue in effect.

Law and jurisdiction

This disclaimer will be governed by and construed in accordance with Swiss law, and any disputes relating to this disclaimer will be subject to the exclusive jurisdiction of the courts of Switzerland.

INTRODUCTION

The Internet, used on a daily basis by personal users, as well as by commercial companies and organizations, includes all sites and portals that are indexed by a public web browser.

These sites and portals are connected with each other via the incoming and outgoing links. These pages are crawled by indexing robots using links that lead to them and links that lead from them to other websites.

These pages are expected to be static, installed on the servers and to have visible html code. Any change to the web portal or any page results with new content being uploaded to the server. In this way, the entire process is visible and public. Another feature of the Internet is the DNS (Domain Name System) database, which associates hostnames with their IP addresses.

DNS databases are defined and used to enable transparency, to control the flow of information and to protect users from spam or certain contents. Increasing control and monitoring of Internet users in terms of information and content they publish and portals that visit, has led to development of a different version of the Internet, where the degree of anonimity is higher.

Many users are aware that everything that is published on the Internet remains permanently visible in some form. That is why even the average user comes to the idea that at least for some of the activities should use so-called dark Web, or deep Web. DARKNET is a general network which can be accessed only by using specific software, configuration, or with the authorization, often using non-standard communication protocols and ports.

Unlike static pages from the indexed part of the Internet (visible Internet), DARKNET pages are dynamic, with html code created based on results of contents retrieved from their own databases. This method for creating independent web site makes crawling this site imposible for indexing robots. Precisely, this is one of the reasons why these pages remain non-indexed by the public Internet browser.

From another side DARKNET weba sites contain rich content used for routine communication and propaganda dissemination. These forums contain static and dynamic text files, archive files, and various forms of multimedia. Collection of such diverse-content types introduces many unique challenges not encountered with standard spidering of indexable files. On a related note, a Dark Web forum crawler also must assess the merits of various collection-update strategies.

It is for this reason that the idea of high degree of anonymity in communication and work was used by malicious users in order to address the various illegal activities, from rental services, through drug trafficking and weapons, to human trafficking.

The paper is organized as follows. The second part shows the theoretical background of deep web and dark web, different ways of accessing as well as similarities and differences with the visible part of the Internet. The third part presents examples of the use of DARKNET services, from the user perspective.

Also, examples of different illegal activities that can be found by searching DARKNET are presented. The fourth part discusses the key conclusions of this study. Last section provides a list of references used to gather information about DARKNET and illegal activities on it.

CHAPTER 1

WHAT IS DARKNET

In the literature and everyday use, when referring to non-indexed part of the Internet two terms are intertwined: DARKNET is a term that encompasses everything that Google and other public Internet browsers are not indexing, and therefore can not be returned as search result.

These may be trivial, such as comments on the forums that can be accessed only by registered users, Facebook posts that are set so that only friends can see, private YouTube content which can be accessed only via forwarded link. Also, academic articles that require subsription fee in order to gain access, as well as many other similar item.

Dark Web is a certain amount of content on the deep web used for promotion or distribution of illegal activities. Web sites that allow dealing with illegal activities are mostly hidden behind onion web domain and can be accessed using special search engines.

DARKNET is almost completely anonymous, and it is therefore used by groups that want to remain hidden from the government institutions and agencies in charge of law enforcement. To further protect the users of such systems, money transactions are performed using a specially created digital currency called Bitcoin. Creation and encryption of the currency is supported by the organization that manages the payment, bitcoins transfer and their conversion into conventional money flows.

One of the ways to access DARKNET is Tor (The Onion Router) network, whose primary purpose is to serve as a gateway to this part of the Internet. To hide the address of the Internet user, Tor redirect signals through nearly 6,000 servers.

So as to create a private and secure connection inside the Tor network, the client application incrementally builds a connection between the source and destination of data packets, which consists of encrypted connection between randomly selected server nodes.

This relationship occurs in steps, so that individual server knows only from which server packets are received and to which server they should be forwarded. This is achieved by using a special key for encryption at every step. Once the connection is established it is possible to transmit different types of data using different software packages.

Apart from Tor-a which is in most cases used to share files, I2P (Invisible Internet Project) network layer is used to provide anonymous communication between applications. This layer supports a variety of protocols and applications. Each established connection between two users is being protected using special encryption. The comparison of functionality and security offered by Tor and I2P has shown that I2P is more resistant to attacks by analyzing traffic flow data.

Freenet is another similar solution that is simpler and more convenient use by the broad masses. Access is done from the browser, while in the background the application establishes a connection. The user can choose the level of security on the network. All the communication and sharing of files is via P2P, and every time one establishes the connection, new path is created. For this reason, every reopening of pages takes more time than in the case with the other aforementioned sector and technologies.

The police fact that close to 300,000 Germans are using some form of access DARKNET network testifies to the popularity of this service. The data show that, at global level, more than three million users access the content of dark web. If we compare the amount of data stored in the dark web, it is forty times larger than the visible part of the web and is about 750 terabytes. The entire content is mostly stored in specific databases, as property of the organizations and individuals. Based on this, the visible part of web is about 4%, while the remaining 96% belong to the deep web.

CHAPTER 2

EXAMPLES OF THE USE OF DARKNET SERVICES

In different types of researches five categories of terroristic activities on the Internet are identified. Those categories are: propaganda (to disseminate radical messages), recruitment and training (to encourage people to join the Jihad or other terrorist organizations, and get online training), fundraising (to transfer funds, conduct credit card fraud and other money laundering activities), communications (to provide instruction, resources, and support via email, digital photographs, and chat session), and targeting (to conduct online surveillance and identify vulnerabilities of potential targets such as airports). Besides these categories, DARKNET services are in use for many other abuses.

Some of the examples collected from different sources are described in following paragraphs.

One of the examples of the dark web usage disclosed by the competent anti-drug entities is a portal for drug and other illegal goods trafficking called Silk Road. Its founder and owner was Ross Ulbrich, 29 year old programmer, who introduced himself under a pseudonym Dread Pirate Roberts. Ample evidence was found on his laptop.

From 2011 to 2013 he created an empire worth $ 1.2 billion, only with the help of a laptop and the Internet. After only three weeks of trial, the jury of twelve declared Ulbricht guilty on all seven counts, including one on charges of money laundering, drug trafficking and computer hacking. He was discovered when the police found his message from 2010 where, at the time of carelessness, he was referring interested parties to visit the Silk Road, signed a different name ("altoid"), under which he sought professionals in bitcoin community to be the leading developers, and gave the address for communication.

This site was operated like any other portal for online purchases. Ordered goods were delivered by postal companies. Postal companies do not check the contents of the shipment in order to provide better services to users, making this method of delivery a very convinient way for illegal trade. At the same time postal company can face problems if the competent authorities establish that the it is often used for these types of delivery.

The elentlessness of people who deal with this kind of crime is evidenced by the fact that only a month after Ulbrich arrest and closing of the portal, portal became active again in the dark web, this time in version 2.0. The site quickly expanded and, according to data from the FBI, had an average of 150,000 visitors and monthly income of around $ 8 million from the sale of goods and services. After a year's work site was shut down, while the administrator Blake Benthall arrested.

That lasted only an hour, after which portal was started again and continued to work, this time in version 3.0. This fact demonstrates the strength of dark web and stability of portals on it.Until 2012, the Silk Road owned a sister site - The Armory, which specializes in trade of firearms, blunt and sharp object for injuring and killing.

The same site went off due to poor attendance after a period of time. Sales of weapons and ammunition is carried out in a similar manner across other sites, some of which guarantee the delivery around the globe, under the motto "We deliver globally, because all people have the right to protection themselves".

Everithing can be found, from pistols to C4 explosives. Delivery is made in special packages so that they can pass x-ray inspection, or often packed in toys, various other instruments and electrical appliances.

There are a number of examples where children were used for geining money.

During 2011, Europol, in coordination with thirteen different countries, arrested 184 people suspected of child abuse and the spread of children pornography in form of images. A similar campaign was carried out in the UK. In this action 650 people accused of different forms of child abuse, from possession of child pornography images to pandering were arrested In 2015, on the territory of Northern Ireland 37 people were arrested based on charges of pedophilia and distribution of child pornography using Tor.

There are examples showing that DARKNET is the perfect place for Cyber Crime.

Users here can buy a variety of malware. At the same time, visitors of websites can become victims of various types of malware, distributed using phishing. One of such malware is vawtrak - banking Trojan distributed via e-mail (Sancho, 2015). Another large group of malware that can be found on the DARKNET are the CryptoLocker malwares. These malware, after accessing victim files, perform the encryption. After encrypting files, the victim is being redirected to a page where it is asked to make the payment if they want to re-gain control of their data. Very often the request for payment and information necessary to complete the transactions are written in the native language of the victim. The role of Tor in these transactions is hosting sites for payment in order to execute transactions using bitcoins.

In addition to malware, interested parties can use DARKNET to hire hackers to carry out various types of hacker attacks on their behalf. Depending on the complexity and risk of the task, rates range from a few dozen to several thousand dollars. They offer a variety of services, from correcting assessment in schools through the theft of access codes for different functions and sensitive autorithative data. The Chinese group Hidden Lynx claims to have up to hundreds of professional cyber thieves, who broke into the computer systems of Google, Adobe and Lockheed Martin.

For people with more sinister intentions and serious willingness to go down in the dark world of the dark web, there are also services of professional assassins. One of the examples described in describes a person with moral and highly flexible business principles, supposedly verified mercenary "with eight-year experience" which offers services which are exclusively paid forward in Bitcoin's. During the contact with such persons, onlyexchanging information on the victim is allowed. The requirement is that all communications, as well as any contact by email must be encrypted. If any part of the communication is not encrypted, it will be deleted.

Another portal that offers such services is known as Lovecraft. The ad states that the members of the organization are former soldiers and mercenaries of Foreign Legion. Moto of this organization is "The best place to store your problem is grave." This portal pays great attention to the protection and privacy of customer communications.

Name, home and work address, as many photos and information about who the victim lives, license plate, description and picture of the vehicle used are informations needed about the target. Depending on the agreement, a team of killers states to prepare for a job, travel, locating and tracking targets require about two months, and the cost of purchasing airline tickets, weapons and accommodation, are not included the initial price.

One portal called C'thulu offers different ways of murdering, from regular through torture and rape, to the bombing. Prices of services range from $ 3,000 to $ 180,000 depending on the chosen category and social status of the victim. Price, of course, differ on whether that person to be killed belonged to the masses, or is a public figure, a politician, a member of law enforcement, etc.

In the DARKNET, counterfeit money can be bought. In addition to the money, a guarantee is almost always given, as well as the description of the creation process showing that, as the sellers say, the counterfeit money is created in the same way as real money. All currencies that are worth falsified are available, but the quality and quantity vary. In these types of transactions, it is common for 600 US dollars to obtain 2,500 counterfeit, a 500 euro 2,000 counterfeit. All transactions are carried out with the promise that they can undergo standard checks, including that of ultraviolet light In many cases, of course, pay for the counterfeit money uses Bitcoin.

Stolen information about the different accounts, credit card numbers, numbers of bank accounts, online auctions can also be purchased. Atlantic Carding is a location in a DARKNET where you can buy information about other people's credit cards, addresses and related personal information. Prices range between 5 and 80 dollars. The quality of information depends on the price. On the other hand, accounts sale is done in one of two ways.

The first method involves the purchase of a single account, provided detailed information on the amount of funds on it. Another way involves the purchase of large quantities of accounts, of which a certain number probably valid. The first method is far more cost-effective, because the customer has insight into the amount of funds in the account, providing better guarantee that the funds invested will be recovered, and the extra money earned. In addition, there is the possibility of buying physical debit and credit cards of different banks.

There are several sites on the DARKNET claiming to selling passports and identity documents. Price of these services depends on the country in which the documents are produced, as well as from the seller. The validity of these documents is difficult to verify, especially when it comes to citizenship. These services can also be created for fraud for immigrants who want citizenship of the country in which they are located at all costs. For example, price for passports, driving licenses and identity cards for Australia is 800 euros at portal called Fake ID. At the same portal, the most expensive document are for USA and the cheapest for Malaysia.

In addition to the above, the more bizarre things can be found on the DARKNET, such as trafficking in human organs. According to the some websites, the kidney can be purchased for $ 200,000, heart for 120,000, liver for 150,000, a pair of eyes to 1,500 US dollars. In addition, various beauty products from human flesh and skin can be purchased. Also, it is possible to find a vide variety of topics that meet the various fetishes. Some of these contents are horrific footage of last conversation and words of passengers in a crashing plane, a prisoners on the day of execution (for example, the electric chair in prison in Texas) or pornographic materials in which women gauze small animals with heels. Different offers in which people offer themselves as food or other types of cannibalism also can be found. In the dark web there is well known portal reffered as Red Room, the place where the torture and killing of people are shown via live stream.

Terrorists also share ideologies on the Web that provide religious commentaries to legitimize their actions. Based on a study of 172 members participating in the global Salafi Jihad, it is concluded that the Internet has created a concrete bond between individuals and a virtual religious community. Web appeals to isolated individuals by easing loneliness through connections to people sharing some commonality. Such virtual community offers a number of advantages to terrorists. It no longer ties to any nation, fostering a priority of fighting against the far enemy (e.g., the United States) rather than the near enemy.

Internet chat rooms tend to encourage extreme, abstract, but simplistic solutions, thus attracting most potential Jihad recruits who are not Islamic scholars. The anonymity of Internet cafes also protects the identity of terrorists. However, Internet can not be in a direct contact with Jihad, because devotion to Jihad must be fostered by an intense period of face-to-face interaction (Chen, Chung, Qin, Reid, Sageman, & Weimann, 2008). In addition, existing studies about terrorists' use of the Web mostly use a manual approach to analyze voluminous data. Such an approach does not scale up to rapid growth of the Web and frequent change of terrorists'identities on the Web.

One of terrorist web sites Alneda.com identified by the U.S. Government called itself the "Center for Islamic Studies and Research," and provided information for Al Qaeda (Thomas, 2003). To group members, terrorists use the Web to share motivational stories and descriptions of operations. To mass media and non-members, they provide analysis and commentaries of recent events on their Web sites. For example, Azzam. com urged Muslims to travel to Pakistan and

Afghanistan to fight the "Jewish-backed American Crusaders". Another web site Qassam.net appealed for donations to purchase AK-47 rifles.

Web portals on the DARKNET are protected in various ways. One of the main ways is to check the behavior of visitors who do not follow the standard pattern. If administrators recognize suspect behaviour of visitors they launch a basic check. Surveillance can be identified if a visitor can see only active row in the text, but no previous rows.

The next step is to put the so-called key logger program on visitors computer, so as to record everything a visitor keystroke. In this way, maximum control over all visitor activities is achieved until administrators check who the visitors are and what their intentions are.

CHAPTER 3

IS MONITORING THE DARKNET THE BEST WAY TO SLOW DOWN CYBERCRIME?

Cybercrime starts and ends with stolen information.

According to ITProPortal, the cybercrime economy could be bigger than Apple, Google and Facebook combined. The industry has matured into an organized market that is probably more profitable than the drug trade.

Criminals use innovative and state-of-the-art tools to steal information from large and small organizations and then either use it themselves or, most common, sell it to other criminals through the Dark Web.

Small and mid-sized businesses have become the target of cybercrime and data breaches because they don't have the interest, time or money to set up defenses to protect against an attack. Many have thousands of accounts that hold Personal Identifying Information, PII, or intelligent property that may include patents, research and unpublished electronic assets. Other small businesses work directly with larger organizations and can serve as a portal of entry much like the HVAC company was in the Target data breach.

Some of the brightest minds have developed creative ways to prevent valuable and private information from being stolen. These information security programs are, for the most part, defensive in nature. They basically put up a wall of protection to keep malware out and the information inside safe and secure.

Sophisticated hackers discover and use the organization's weakest links to set up an attack

Unfortunately, even the best defensive programs have holes in their protection. Here are the challenges every organization faces according to a Verizon Data Breach Investigation Report in 2013:

- 76 percent of network intrusions explore weak or stolen credentials

- 73 percent of online banking users reuse their passwords for non-financial websites

- 80 percent of breaches that involved hackers used stolen credentials

Symantec in 2014 estimated that 45 percent of all attacks is detected by traditional anti-virus meaning that 55 percent of attacks go undetected. The result is anti-virus software and defensive pro-tection programs can't keep up. The bad guys could already be inside the organization's walls.

Small and mid-sized businesses can suffer greatly from a data breach. Sixty percent go out of business within a year of a data breach according to the National Cyber Security Alliance 2013.

What can an organization do to protect itself from a data breach?

For many years I have advocated the implementation of "Best Practices" to protect personal identifying information within the business. There are basic practices every business should implement to meet the requirements of federal, state and industry rules and regulations. I'm sad to say very few small and mid-sized businesses meet these standards.

The second step is something new that most businesses and their techs haven't heard of or implemented into their protection programs. It involves monitoring the DARKNET.

The DARKNET holds the secret to slowing down cybercrime Cybercriminals openly trade stolen information on the Dark Web. It holds a wealth of information that could negatively impact a businesses' current and prospective clients. This is where criminals go to buy-sell-trade stolen data. It is easy for fraudsters to access stolen information they need to infiltrate business and conduct nefarious affairs. A single data breach could put an organization out of business.

Fortunately, there are organizations that constantly monitor the DARKNET for stolen information 24-7, 365 days a year. Criminals openly share this information through chat rooms, blogs, websites, bulletin boards, Peer-to-Peer networks and other black market sites. They identify data as it accesses criminal command-and-control servers from multiple geographies that national IP addresses cannot access. The amount of compromised information gathered is incredible. For example:

Millions of compromised credentials and BIN card numbers are harvested every month Approximately one million compromised IP addresses are harvested every day. This information can linger on the DARKNET for weeks, months or, sometimes, years before it is used. An organization that monitors for stolen information can see almost immediately when their stolen information shows up. The next step is to take proactive action to clean up the stolen information and prevent, what could become, a data breach or business identity theft. The information, essentially, becomes useless for the cybercriminal.

What would happen to cybercrime when most small and mid-sized businesses take this Dark Web monitoring seriously?

The effect on the criminal side of the DARKNET could be crippling when the majority of businesses implement this program and take advantage of the information. The goal is to render stolen information useless as quickly as possible.

There won't be much impact on cybercrime until the majority of small and mid-sized businesses implement this kind of offensive action. Cybercriminals are counting on very few businesses take proactive action, but if by some miracle businesses wake up and take action we could see a major impact on cybercrime.

Cleaning up stolen credentials and IP addresses isn't complicated or difficult once you know that the information has been stolen. It's the businesses that don't know their information has been compromised that will take the biggest hit.

Is this the best way to slow down cybercrime? What do you this is the best way to protect against a data breach or business identity theft - Option one: Wait for it to happen and react, or Option two: Take offensive, proactive steps to find compromised information on the Dark Web and clean it up?

IS IT SAFE TO BROWSE THE DARKNET?

- It depends upon the factor that you try to access inside the DARKNET underworld. A lot of legal and illegal content available on the DARKNET websites. It is 100% safe to surf the legal content.

- But, if you try to access the illegal content or trying to buy or sell any illegal stuff like drugs, weapons, hitman service, etc., then you will get busted.

- If you want to be safe on the dark web, use our strongest NordVPNthat is most recommended by our com. Also, compare the other powerful VPN (virtual private network) available on the internet.

HOW BIG IS THE DARKNET?

- It is unimaginable. You can't predict the size of the dark web.
- Almost every information is hidden in the web which can't be indexed or fetch or crawled by Googlebot or any other search engines.

- There is a marketplace in the dark/deep web where you can buy and sell drugs, guns, adult contents etc.

- There are much more things available on the DARKNET than the normal web.

- If you start digging the internet on the surface, you probably could get only a 4% of the information.

- But there is a deeper inside the web called Deep/Dark web, where you can get a lot more networked web pages.

- About 96% of information is hidden on the DARKNET underworld.

- It includes legal and illegal stuff.

_ADVANTAGES:

- Anonymity (Anonymity results in freedom) is one of the greatest benefits of the Darknet markets. Nobody has to know your name if you want to purchase an illegal item.

- For instance, if users want to buy drugs on these anonymous online marketplaces, they will likely find cheaper products than the one on the streets. Also, vendors are willing to offer a discount if customers are buying in bulk.
- No physical contactwith vendors is another important reason why people choose DARKNET rather than buying products on the street. Users don't have to be afraid that someone will see them or they'll get arrested while buying the product.
- You can buy many products that are not available in your country. Some items being sold on Darknet markets cannot be found in every country. Not easily, People can find almost every drug there is, and it is just one click away.
- Convenience is another reason why people tend to order drugs and weapons from Darknet vendors. Users don't have to look for a dealer or drive to buy the product. Everything they need can be done from the

comfort of their home, and the product will arrive to your shipping address in no time.

- The good thing about Darknet marketplaces is a strong community. Users can share their experience and give advice about certain vendor
- Transfer any amount without any tax.
- Can start business by bit coin.
- Privacy
- Freedom of speech

DISADVANTAGES:

People who buy products on the DARKNET should always keep in mind that they can never be too safe and they can get into a lot of trouble with the law. For buying drugs, one can be fined and even end up in jail. You have to follow all of the guidelines regarding the Tor browser if you want to avoid getting arrested. Also, make sure to use proper VPN protocol. Nonetheless, if the user wants to buy a weapon to commit a terroristic act, they can end up in prison for life.

Customers can never be sure that the stuff they order is the stuff they'll get.What they can do is order products from trustful Storing money in online walletsis another downside of buying products on the DARKNET markets. Users should always keep their bitcoins in their personal wallets until they are ready to purchase an item.

Shipment seizingis always a risk factor if your order has to cross an international border. Also, the risk of you or your vendor getting caught increases.

There is a great possibility that occasional problems with some DARKNET markets might happen. Some markets can be down for a month.

Another downside of buying products on the DARKNET , especially drugs, is that you can never check the quality of the product. Once the product arrives, in most cases there is no way you can get your money back.

The only thing you can do is to leave a negative review for the vendor.

Negative Content – One problem visitors to the Deep Web, also known as the Dark Web, experience is negative content. Types of material that are filtered out of normal search engines are readily available; many of the pages on the DARKNET display illegal content related to drugs, violence, private information or pornography.

CONCLUSION:

If you want to purchase something on the Dark Web you should always weigh in possible consequences.

Even though it is not completely safe, and users can be punished if caught, millions of customers are still buying products on the Darknet market places.

The reason for that is anonymity and a wide range of available items.

If you want to be safe while browsing the Dark Web, you should always use proper VPN protocol, and follow all the guidelines that Tor recommends such as:

- Don't use your browser in full-screen
- Don't use Skype or any other program that can cause your
- IP address to leak.